I'm a Pretty Little Black Girl Traveling 'Round the World

D0889420

Azalea Jordan

Copyright © 2022 Azalea Jordan

ISBN: 9798836918651

CONTENTS

ACKNOWLEDGMENTS

I wrote this book because I want to show people how fun traveling can be. Some people never leave their city. I hope this book inspires you to go see the world and enjoy your life. There is so much to see.

AROUND THE WORLD I WILL GO

Around the world I will go,
taking adventures far and wide. Come and see what
adventures went down with my family and I!

I WAS BORN TO TRAVEL

This is me. Azalea Jordan. I was only 8-weeks old when my parents marched me down to the passport office and got me my first passport. I am now working on filling up my second passport.

I like to say that I was born to travel. I love traveling. I love getting on airplanes (I especially love the personal televisions screens and the food). I love exploring new places and cultures (especially the food). In this book I will take you to the places I've traveled to so far in my ten years on this planet.

BARBADOS

Welcome to Barbados!
I travelled here when I
was only 8 months
old. This was my first
stamp in my passport.

Barbados Facts:

The grapefruit
originated in
Barbados.

You can visit one of
the 18 last
remaining Concorde
planes at the
airport.

Cattlewash Beach in
St Andrew is known
for its healing
properties.

Holetown was the
first settlement in
Barbados.

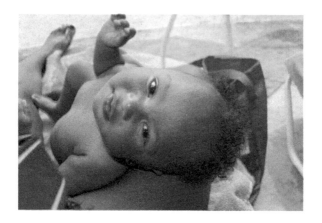

My dad's family is from Barbados.

In this picture we were at a cousin's house in the countryside.

Travel Tips:

Traveling to Barbados between July and November will allow you to attend Crop Over Festival activities on the island. The temperature during this time is between mid-70s and mid-80s. Peak travel time is from late December to mid-April.

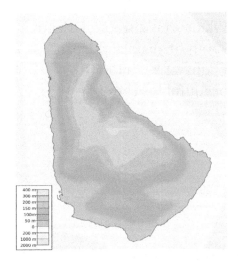

When visiting the island, you must go to Oistin's Friday night fish fry. It is on the beach and has many Bajan food options. People from Barbados are called Bajans.

Definitely try the rotis in Barbados. My dad says that Barbados has the best rotis in all of the Caribbean.

OKINAWA, JAPAN

I first traveled to Japan when I was one year old. We went to visit my mom's childhood friend in Okinawa, Japan. I call her "Auntie Karen." Okinawa is a tropical island south of mainland Japan. Okinawa has a lot of beautiful beaches.

My mom grew up in Japan so she showed us all around Okinawa when we go there. She loves the beach so we spent a lot of time at the beach.

This was my dad's first time in Japan too. My mom went to elementary school on Mainland Japan, but went to middle school and high school in Okinawa, Japan.

WE MOVED TO JAPAN...TWICE

After that visit, we moved to Okinawa, Japan when I was three years old. We lived there for a year and a half that time. Finally, we moved to Iwakuni, Japan when I was nine years old. I currently live in Japan. I'll talk more about that later.

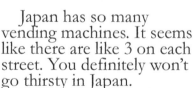

Japan has so many vending machines. It seems like there are like 3 on each street. You definitely won't go thirsty in Japan.
In Okinawa there is a drink called apple tea, too. You can find it in almost all the drink vending machines.

KINDERGARTEN IN JAPAN

Kindergarten in Japan is called yochien. I went to yochien when my family moved to Japan. I was the only Black girl in my class. My mom would braid my hair with beads. The Japanese students always wanted to touch my hair. My mom also dressed me in Doc McStuffins a lot because she wanted Japanese kids to see that Black kids had popular characters too. She said she also wanted me to feel good about being a Black girl in Japan.

My dad's mom came to visit us in Okinawa and got to see my school.

My sister and I went to the same school. Yochien is two years in Japan. My brother goes to yochien now. So all three of us went to Japanese school.

This was my yochien.

We don't wear outside shoes inside the school. Why? We don't we wear shoes inside the school to avoid getting the floor dirty.

Above my shoes is my name in Japanese. I can read and write in two Japanese written languages, Hiragana and Katakana. I can read some Kanjis. My name above is written in Katakana.

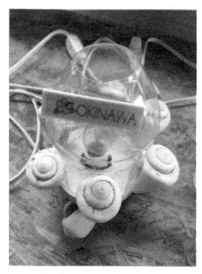

Fun facts about Okinawa:

- Okinawa is a prefecture in Japan. Prefecture is what Japan calls its states.
- Okinawa made up of coral rock.
- Okinawa is made up of hundreds of surrounding islands.
- Okinawan's have their own language but most speak Japanese or a dialect called Hogen.

HONOLULU, HAWAII

When I was in Hawaii I got to see turtles lay their eggs on the beach and then return to the ocean.

I went to the Dole pineapple farm and ate ice cream. We also visited my mom and dad's friends and they took us all around the big island.

Fun facts about Hawaii:

Surfing was invented in Hawaii. Now people surf all over the world.

You can mail a coconut from here.

Maui's Mount Haleakala is the largest dormant volcano in the whole entire world.

In Hawaii, you can wear white pants after Labor Day (I had to ask my mom what this meant. Who knew this was a. thing).

Hawaii is the only U.S. state with two official languages.

SOUTH AFRICA

My family and I visited my Godparents in Stellenbosch, South Africa when I was four years old. We visited Cape Town, went up to Table Mountain, visited a botanical garden, and we went on a safari. I got to see penguins on the coast of South Africa and a whale too!

My cousin Kiana, my sister Zaya, and me at the airport traveling to South Africa. Kiana was 9 years old, Zaya was only 2 years old and I was 4 years old.

Us on the airplane
going to South Africa.

We saw these lions when
we went on the safari.

These are the
penguins we saw in
South Africa. Did you
know that South Africa
is close to Antartica so
the ocean there is cold?

My cousin and I riding the bus up to Table Mountain.

An interesting fact about South Africa:

South Africa's seasons are opposite of the seasons in the United States. So, when it is summer in the United States, it is Winter in South Africa. When it is fall in the United States, it is spring in South Africa. I always say that one year I want to have my birthday in South Africa so I can have a warm birthday.

AMSTERDAM, NETHERLANDS

This was my first time in Europe. We spent a day traveling around Amsterdam on our way home from South Africa. It was cold there. I saw a lot of people riding bikes. We rode on a river boat and floated past the place where Anne Frank wrote her journal.

Facts about Amsterdam:

Amsterdam is the capital of the Netherlands. It has about 7000 momental buildings.

There is a famous floating flower market in Amsterdam. Flowers get delivered by boat.

Amsterdam has a lot of water running through it. There are 165 canals in Amsterdam. Well, and because there is so much water, there are 1281 bridges in Amsterdam.

Finally, there are more bikes in Amsterdam than there are people.

LONDON, ENGLAND

When I was six years old I traveled to London with my family. I was so excited to be getting on the airplane again!

This was my little brother, Zayden's first international trip. My sister and I were helpers on the journey.

I remember seeing a lot of old buildings in London. We went on a huge ferris wheel called The London Eye. We stayed on a military base called Mendenhall Air Force Base.

London had a lot of old buildings. We walked the streets and looked at them. We actually did a lot of walking in London.

My dad's military job is why we went to London. I am a military child. Being a military child is pretty cool because you can travel to new places and experience new things. Some military children move around a lot.

Facts about London:

Did you know there are over 300 languages spoken in London?

London is the capital of England and the United Kingdom.

London is the smallest city in England.

London is one of the most diverse cities in the world.

There are a lot of free museums in London.

London is famous for fish and chips, but there are so many different types of cultures in London that you can find almost any type of food there.

The London Zoo was the first zoo in the world.

London hosted the olympics 3 times.

When we traveled to London, I was in a track club. While I was in London I practiced my running at the track on the military base. My mom used to call me "ZaZa Zoom."

We traveled to the ocean and looked to see if we could see France across this body of water. Of course we couldn't.

We found a skating rink while we were in England. That was pretty fun.

I went to real tea house!

When we went to the tea house, it was so exciting! I had to be on my best behavior and act like a princess ! (Afternoon tea is generally served around **3 or 4 p.m.** these days.)

YES, I TRAVEL THE STATES TOO.

So far I have talked about me traveling with my family to places outside of the United States of America. I want to take a minute to name some of the placed I've been to within the United States.

Reno, Nevada. Having fun in the snow.

San Antonio, Texas

Tacoma, Washington
Visiting my Opa & Mama Toni

Oklahoma City, Oklahoma
Visiting my Great Great Auntie.

Las Vegas, Nevada

Washington, DC
President Obama's
Inauguration

ANAHEIM, CALIFORNIA

I love Disney! I've been to Disneyland in California many times. This time is one of my favorites because I paid for my own ticket with money I earned from my business. When I have enough money I want to go to Disneyland in Tokyo, Japan again but this time with my friends.

ALBUQUERQUE, NEW MEXICO

I went to the hot air balloon festival and it was amazing! If you have never been, you must see this with your own eyes. All the bright colors on the balloons.

YOSEMITE NATIONAL PARK

The trip to Yosemite National Park was a very fun time. We went to the Mirror Lake. Did you know that Mirror Lake is only ankle deep? We also hiked some trails. My family hikes during the summer time. We saw some rivers and waterfalls as well. Finally, did you know some of the tallest trees in the world are in Yosemite National Park? They are called The Grizzly Giant Sequoia.

I've been to Disneyland in California many times. I have also been to Disneyland in Tokyo, but this was my first time in Disney World.

We rode so many rides. I loved the Avatar ride. We wore googles and rode on something that looked like a motorcycle. It was a virtual reality ride.

I liked Disney World because it had four different sections and resorts. We actually stayed at a Disney Resort. We stayed there four days. Each day we went to one of the different park.

The different parks at Disney World are
Disney's Hollywood Studios, Disney's Animal
Kingdom, Magic Kingdom, and Epcot. We went to
the Celebration of the Lion King performance at
Africa in Animal Kingdom and it was awesome!

GRAND CANYON, ARIZONA

Before the COVID pandemic, we had a trip to Singapore planned and it was canceled due to the pandemic. I was sad about that. Covid didn't stop me from traveling though. My mom always says, "what CAN we do?" So, my mom and dad took us on a roadtrip to see the Grand Canyon when we couldn't travel many other places.

When we went to the Grand Canyon, we didn't do it alone. We had our homeschool friends go with us, and we also had our cousin Kiana with us, too. My favorite thing about the Grand Canyon was when I saw people on horses going down in the canyon. It looked scary, but pretty fun.

Fun facts about the Grand Canyon:

Did you know that the Grand Canyon was formed by the Colorado river about 6 million years ago?

There are Over 1000 Caves at the canyon.

The canyon creates its own weather.

Spanish explorers first visited the canyon in the 1540s.

The Havasupai Native Americans Live in the Grand Canyon.

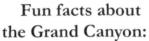

Did you know that the Grand Canyon is bigger than the state Rhode Island? It is the most visited national parks in the United States.

MY CURRENT HOME…IWAKUNI, JAPAN

I live in Iwakuni, Japan. I moved to Iwakuni during the COVID-19 Pandemic. My mom got a job in Iwakuni, Japan. This was a new adventure for my family.

In these pictures we were traveling to our new home, Iwakuni, Japan.

I love the Japanese culture especially Japanese food. I love yakiniku and sushi. The picture above is my mom, sister, brother, and I eating yakiniku. My dad was deployed. Look at all the ice cream flavors down below.

These pictures are taken at the Kintai Bridge. The Kintai has five arches. Many people like to go to this bridge to see the cherry blossoms when they bloom.

We do a lot of hiking in the summer time in Iwakuni. There are a lot of mountains around us. When we lived in Okinawa there was not a lot of mountains. We also camp in the summer time.

Iwakuni is in the Yamaguchi Prefecture. A prefecture is like a state. Next to the Yamaguchi Prefecture is the Hiroshima Prefecture. We travel to other prefectures to explore Japan.

Iwakuni is different from Okinawa where I used to live. In Okinawa it doesn't snow in winter time. It is actually very hot in the winter. In Iwakuni, it can snow a lot. It doesn't snow like Canada snow, but it does snow. Two things Okinawa and Iwakuni have in common are the summer heat and beaches.

DUBAI, UNITED ARAB EMIRATES

Burj, Khalifa - Dubai, United Emirates

I traveled from Japan to Dubai with my family.

My favorite part of flying.

Waiting for our flight.

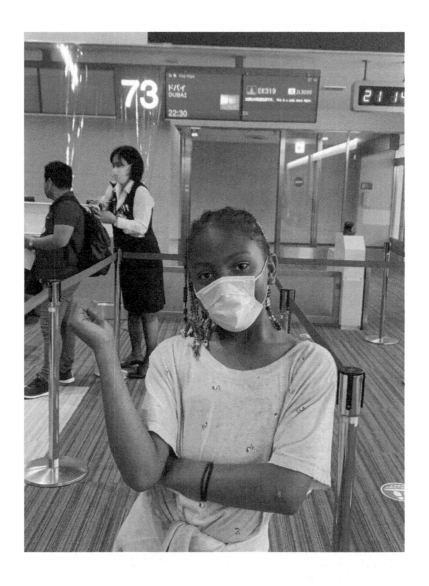

I said to my mom: "Why aren't we traveling in business class? When I grow up, I will be a billionaire and travel 1st class." #goals

Let me tell you, Dubai was HOT! It was 104 degrees on the day we took this picture. This picture was outside of the Dubai Mall.

This was at the Dubai Mall.

This is a mosque. A mosque is a house of prayer for Muslim people. There are over 1400 mosques in Dubai.

Down below is a picture in the Metro station. We rode the Metro around Dubai.

We ate Pakistani food in Dubai. It was delicious. Did you know that the Pakistani population is higher than the Emirati population in Dubai?

PORT LOUIS, MAURITIUS, AFRICA

This my second time in Africa. This time we went to a tropical island country called Mauritius. Mauritius is down by Madagascar.

It was a long trip to Mauritius.

We spent a lot of time at the pool. I met a lot people. I met a girl from India who spoke four languages. I met two kids from South Africa who were also on vacation.

I went parasailing with my family in Mauritius. It was scary at first, but it was beautiful. I thought I was going to have to land in the water but we didn't. We landed on the boat. I went up in the parachute with my grandmother.

I got to spend a lot of time with my family. My grandmother met us in Mauritius and I got to spend quality time with her.

I also got to go to my mom's Soror's wedding. It was my first time going to a wedding and my first time being in a wedding.

We went to a market and drank coconut water straight from a coconut.

We went to a wildlife park where we went on a safari and a roller coaster ride.

This is a Hindu temple in Mauritius. Mauritius has an Indian influence in the country because when Mauritius was colonized by the British, they brought in Indian labor.

Below is a mosque in Mauritius.

I have been on the go since I was born. The adventures will not stop here. I am grateful for the opportunity to travel. I know that my life has been filled with privilege. My parents say that with privilege comes responsibility.

ABOUT THE AUTHOR

I am a ten year old honor roll student going into the fifth grade. I want to be a performing artist when I grow up. Every year I complete a CEO Academy Project where I earn money by creating a business. I give, save, and spend the proceeds.

WHAT'S NEXT?

My travel bucket list includes:

- Nigeria
- Brazil
- Alaska
- South Korea
- Guam
- France
- Australia
- Universal Studios Florida

Made in the USA
Las Vegas, NV
19 August 2022

53614253R00046